HELLOSUNSHINE

HELLOSUNSHINE

BY RYAN ADAMS

This is a work of fiction. All names, characters, places, and incidents are a product of the author's imagination. Any resemblance to real events or persons, living or dead, is entirely coincidental.

Published by Akashic Books
©2009 Ryan Adams

Paperback ISBN-13: 978-1-933354-95-8
Paperback Library of Congress Control Number: 2009924489

Hardcover ISBN-13: 978-1-933354-96-5
Hardcover Library of Congress Control Number: 2009925384

Akashic Books
PO Box 1456
New York, NY 10009
info@akashicbooks.com
www.akashicbooks.com

for bug,
always

Table of Contents

CHAPTER 1

Florida

florida lay there before us
swollen
this driver and me
rolling into a sure ghetto
neon jacksonville ghetto
to get a car
taxi was rattling smoke
shot up with seats ripped
we rolled into the lot
and
streetlamp-outlined men
standing up in a row
braced
each on a corner
body language loud
saying listen they had it
firearms
street pharmaceuticals
and
when our eyes met
palms
blurred

smokeburns
electrical fires
sky ripping those whitecotton
clouds up
in some deep-ass blue
the too-deep sea
never-going-to-see-land-again deep
sky
lost-at-sea deep sky blur
just over there
that
i could see total anger moans
calm rage
lamps without shades
drywall tears
a history of night hours
and
in that moment
some clenched fists
they broke my bones
like
a light
falling off a night table
and like the rats we all are
   florida
florida spat me out
but
i kept my breath

s l o w
a little girl at the bottom of the stairs
scowled
surrounded by night shade
shadow wall bricks
hidden in a mossy stale
funk
in a row on the second floor
landing
in the cement block apartment rise
some half-dressed bodies lit
up
christmas trees these men
were
streetlamp damp
sweating hard
guns near
in the nightpools
she
stared through me
like i was meat
she
held a plastic uzi
in a room staring
like they were eating through my skin
and
without a nod
without a tip

we slid very quietly into the butterscotch
grand prix
the driver and me
under the moons
screaming inside maybe
inside the rooms
with television blurs
circling us and circling it
that car
all armor-alled up and smelling like grease
and
like bad stuff or like something
like forget it
we got in
all of a sudden
he stopped asking me about the money
which was scary
he knew
i knew
he knew
i had that money
and
in your mind you go bloody feet
barely alive screaming for your neighborhood life
out of that place
but
she called
and

he answered
and
something pulled him triggered his heart
click
guiding him smiling to the freeway
no taxi
his nephew's car
butterscotch grand prix
and
off the highway in a
fast food parking lot
the driver pulled me in
hands over my shrugging
sides
delivered me like a wish
as i forked over a little more than bargained
forgot about landing in the wrong city
   that airport dry rotting
forgot about meeting her father
   her father so decent his grill smoking
forgot about the mosquito bites
   pine halls those castle walls of wood
forgot about myself
and
i was just happy to be home
i was happy
to remember who i really was
and

you know
i see that sky still
it reminds me of a dishrag rolled with heavy dew
and
palmettos exploding oranges
that
florida sky emitting total life
and total death
and
me on the fresh steps to
dropping all the bags
arms out
receiving
my destiny
and
hope
in several phases of doubts
colored
somehow
with love

Fruit-Rotting

once in coins subwayesque
we paid
all the way uptown
back in the skeleton-eye
like,
 "hey hey hey gotta
    keep up now"
somebody would shout
sweating
beautiful
on the shitty rushing chinatown
streets
glistening bodies yellow mash
sunrocked
those days...
but
now we are old and in us
drugs rot
like
we are dirty
like our insides are paying
for our sins and not us

our insides like a cross
fruit-rotting
sun-diving
we are eagles now
         beautiful
  and we
we feast on what we like
  lucky ones
so so lucky so lucky
imagine if one of us,
um, found out
one of our best friends had died
overdose-cop-call on an empty bed
or worse
all of us lied
         more
some of us got free on the dust
falling out of the bags
meant for a sick sunday
         or
one of us betrayed the animals
let loose in the disco metal farm
         we
         are
l u c k y
count-your-wishes-and-stars lucky
now we are old and going for more
we are dirty

like our insides went to work for us
for every night we spent in the throws
throwing up diamonds and trust funds
our souls eternal for those nights
and we felt it
a real disco polaroid
  famous wasted
    eternal buzz
      so rocked
but inside it was all a joke
hahahahaha
    and we
we were a joke just all sped up
  and neon
and ugly
  like sharks
  in shiny dresses
  minus leeches
  us, and our
bowls of fruit
fruitcake-dreaming
  but
full of disco-lies and
fucking each other
disgusting
our souls
shining hard in valhalla
but inside

we were lying
and
while we were not busy with the snake
or the unicorn-rainbow hallucinations
if we sat down for even one moment
we knew
once we got home
our insides
they would pay for our sins
while we sat on the window-bed-nook
under a peach-rind quilt
suffering a loss
       we was
bright and alive once
       we was
   was
but now
now;
    just steeped in self juice
and balloon-popped
yellow-yucked
and fucked up
white-wine dinnered
and
disgusting crossworded
all of us
totally
sucking

and
stuck
our insides like a cross
sun-diving
      and
fruit-rotting

Dope Camera

screaming
  lord knows,
screamed
like as in
screaming
as in
  "sunshine came screaming into the room, bottles empty, lines
under eyes
  where they were broken up and followed into a face"
awful
  rocked so hard i broke the crib
  sneezed so hard i broke a rib
    lost a dog
    couldn't take care of it
    couldn't see
eyes breaking out from
fleshy dope smear
  what
what was anybody doing there?
  pretty
pretty people in there
in that fog land

wasted
in that dock of memory
  i worry about all of them
    and
    i don't know, us
nothing really happened
  cuz
we talked so much
  nobody moved
  inside
  the rooms
the brightlight
midnights
were bloody as a lie
    and
fortune cookies hung over us
like the low gongs
  plus-sized songs
the valley was ripe with flashfires
  and
cement trucks
heavy metal freight cars
on wheels
cemetery skin
smoking with the hookers
on Noplace
and 10th
or whatever street

we made this whole thing up
inside my bedroom
  madness close behind
  it felt like
well
  i swallowed the whole of the world
  in a night
screamed
for the past
to hear me first
  and
take me last
like as in
screaming
as in
scream team m.v.p.
  now totally m.i.a.
  and all, "fuck you"
    somebody really should have had the cameras rolling
    back then
well
some of them did
  oops
our lives went
  bullshitting
with the loansharks
  and
we all bought the tent

golden tooth
paying all the rent
inside
lord knows
we are all...
screaming

Bags

three bags
sit
on this bench
sunlit
flies also
not on the bags
a tree, oak, long branches
reaches behind
ever lit also yellow sunlight
and
green-washed like salt blast
from water reefs
this greenish thing
i walk past
in a moment
thinking
"i am not here"
sure as fire my lover
reclines
and
the electricity pulsing through the grid
in the metal towers racing in a row

through the cut-low grass hills
trees on either side
like
an evergreen racing grid
pump the towns with light
as we read
aloud
the words to the song of our life
in time with the jets
singing
"i know a love
true
and
i know a love
strong"
we know...
and
like a saturday is coming
like
a fucking wall is caving
like all the rest
just easing into it
like
bricks
like
who fucking cares?
me—
three bags sit

on the bench
in the summer
of my dreams
filled with rose petals
filled with candy
i left them there
without reason
no reason
i am beyond reason
really
almost
beyond reason
almost
really
i am
i was

Feverpitch

in a feverpitch the note broke my eyes
so glassed
and in the kitchen i did the dishes very poorly
almost as if to say
to make this last
"i will prolong this"
my battle against time
my unmade bed
moans
so that if i must use these
things
again
they will go under the water
for
things are more useful
clean
like
dreaming
with my eyes closed and
open
either way
i am open

as in

opening

nonstop full-time

sleeping fuzz-faced

overage costs, ratios, house dollars

the build-up

counter tops, numbers, receipts in jars

calculators tick-tock tick-tocking

my body is counting itself

counting something

so many new

pieces

ah, my lungs feel like

what

what ash is

on a still warm backyard summer fire

on strike

fresh-cut grass must feel like this

does it feel

no

burning embers like what that might feel like

to feel

i feel things and i apply metaphor i dunno why i do that

i don't know how to explain my feelings

ever

so i write too much down talkmouth blahzzzrt

too much not enough

man

my nose is running
achoo
it feels like running
there's so much energy in pain
and so much madness in energy
now this!
NOT doing something, so
feverpitch...
there's no sense in
NOT talking
that should be so easy right
how much poison
really
how much extraction
before i'm better
before i say this
"i guess i had enough"
   or YES!
and
   OK THANKS! haha
that note rung so loud
it cracked our porcelain sky
and
it cracked bad pink clouds, goshawks circling
soon
i will put on my colored faces
and planting boots
and

i will go cast myself into the painted desert walls

and sycamore tree fuckery

plus no one but

the coyotes

say, man, say

these animals cannot read

but we remember what overwhelming

REALLY is captain?

...no?

well

a coyote's cry echoes

& hopefully

one day

one last face full of tears

and cracked eyes

will drain simple lines

for a pool of howls

but

glowing

when that note breaks the spell

and

it's curtains

to all things false

to all things sour

and

ill timed

in a feverpitch

for

a hope
i will be here for you, my love
always
   on key
in the dusted halls
   of
the infinite hours
feverpitched
   and
cherrysour

Numbers

Blitzed
all kinds of slow sad
My God
i remember being really pilled out
numb
the TV blew all this static at me about
WAR
because
WAR SELLS like POETRY likes WAR
fuck that
    seriously
i was all pilled up
Medication Station
and this giant love
earth/air elemental
orange-juice-good
for me
and me
numb
her,
right beside me—
white walls

cotton sheets
asleep
and on the f'n TV
Just War Shit
numb
Blitzed
then
then
then i go deaf from this
fucking head trip thing i got
my grandfather, he was also
super deaf/super duper hearing-
aide deaf
now
Now i can't hear the numbers
people's kids are all shot up in
the desert
they only dream this empty sand
trap
and
say the names
and there i was
alone
in my head
going deaf
afraid
i wouldn't be able to hit the notes
and

i would forget the numbers
and
   all these people were dying
all shot up
   my lover asleep
    ready to let me slip away
     across the ocean
      all pilled up
       i got so lucky
        i even got kinda
         religious about it
  Blitzed
all
  numb
My God

OK, Wow

i allow myself the invitation,
i surround the door,
ill at ease,
 maybe—but draped—still
foolishly,
eh
i have a wiry shape...
his
my grandfather's
and
possibly wolves
i dunno
age...
things growing...
backaches
and oh wow
ow
"that hurts"
but
"this feels fine"
certainly
well, "doesn't it

always
something?"
all these things match
the way
i have to always wear a watch
because
it's right to enjoy the race
morning turning day
for
someday
we will meet inside the gates
because
there is nothing left to do
but not be late
and
we all learn from our mistakes
like it or not
ugh,
ouch
and
well,
ok, w o w

I Am Standing on This Beach

i am on this fucking beach.
noisy noisy waves...blast, blast in my face
so loud—
pigeons,
sea spray,
the second crash comes after the first
like a wave—it binds though, so binds
itself to the rot of the beach; a "fuckoff"
almost to the tide... washing garbage on dirty sand-like-sand,
colors—electric blue, with candy wrappers and condoms
and shells/plus some breeze that comes,
goes, comes, goes, oblivious to tempo or
nature even
a beach, on the fucking endless beach
where
that goddamn sun
rises and falls like
a loud boss; like a
nightmare; restart
machine-ball hot
like a nuclear stop
watch

....i watch it.

watch it.......

break into the fall of lines sized for angels and ancient gods or
mountains

—born there,

and...

no matter how it sounds,

crass and underhanded,

inside any man,

fought off or not,

it's just

it's just this...

a woman can be a junk ship, wooden,

patched red sail here and there like

flying over singapore thru that fog

ever there—hiding it.....her/us/me/it

her/me/us/it/fog—

fog—like singapore fog

we are hiding.

sad

sad

sad

(always—then—

like magic—whammo—descend and out the window—there it
is—

beautiful and

not in any time—not decade-era fixed—

"totally" non-american—past/present—

all functioning at once—.......................
with harbors—junk ships—and my, my
god, my god....
all lit with skyscraper xmas lights—
lit peaks and nighttime valleyhouses
a fortress of woven wooden trunks
of trees—blinded by mad mad mad
beauty).....
mad beauty.....
and a man is a tug, mechanical and
plastic; hard-lining sunken; work'd
manhands broken nails chalked palms
boxer-sized
bed-ready—
the kind that fix ropes round boxes
if they had to
with an elephant cargo—before they
were even a child—past sails, deaths, things drunk......ugh,,,,,,,
drunken...worse—beyond youth more
"curse of youth"
all that shit
no matter how mannered
no matter how buddhist
no matter how many dresses
who?
who is handing out the charity turkeys
on new year's
in the mission, low key—crying—with

some lady saying "it's ok honey—we all do it, you just ain't been
down here as long,"
all that shit, in a man,
always,,,,,,,,,
but
whatever really,
a man, hey, he is still a tug
tugboat.
a tug.
and sometimes,
sometimes, not always,
but sometimes,
it needs repair/slides up aside
there—"there" like arms; like long pale arms—
..........................from the junk ship
down come the ropes—to bind
tugboats plastic outsides align—soft
each splinter of wood into the fabric
of shitty-weather salt-riddled plastic
feel like rooms
if a child were born
in the heart of a man
...inside his tug,
his cry machine,
his eyes.
...beaten too—from a weather-only an
ocean-sized dream that never ended
could whisper it to you—///////////rusted

so that you might believe—and you do.
inside the flicker or the blue
no words say shit—just a look
and every horizon-wave-tide—
bloody rope gloved catch—it is.
it just is.
she sees.
in a lucky thought here—she smiles—
but we just don't know.
we don't know what she
or he would really do.
not really...
so
into a bed two could go, harbor side
torn apart—funnily, no different than
any mechanic, working on a car—but
this ocean, he works in it, and it—it—
THAT ocean
it is so many-many-many-many hearts
in a row—what you throw out and what
comes back—never mind so much..........
it's all that bottomless and in-between
that, well, you know,
that is what drives any tug driver home
H O M E
home—
eventually—
that is if a man were lucky.

lucky being fickle,
fickle luck being funny,
funny being sad sometimes,
like you just ran out of it—
steam, money,
dreams, honeycomb
or blankets,
and somebody was going to get cold.
cold,
not in a home.
to know a home
my god,
how lucky.
and certainly a postman too, a diver or
a saloon owner or a personal driver or
anyone,
it drives them home,
this in and out of an ocean of somethings
thoughts, working-assembly-line
working-desk-sitting-phone-answering—
everyone, even those in a dream when
they do a thing—
something in them realizes that clock
upon the wall
if it is to be anything so true
it is just numbers of a face—kind,
beautiful
we are lucky to return to—

our homes...
and
into a bed the bind is not the sizes of a shape of a person there
to hide against
but hopeful blue light if a tv set is on—
or just doors/windows—open to the stars,
or......
impressions of stars cause unnatural
light also binds itself too, like when
it is not a me
or a him or her
or a you
but an us.
where the ocean stops.........................
but it stops.
not home.
no home there.
lucky-not.
noisy noisy waves, tideblast, blast in a face, squinting in
place.........................
sarong or blanket flag flying
horizontal colors
against that line
that goes down the sides
of a woman.
in a wow, sigh,
from sea spray for a little while till the
ocean is the woman who you waited for

and,
strangely, saying this as a man,
why you went,
why you went anyway.......a soldier
of sorts, to collect new things inside
you—
to restart those eyes, that woman, and
without a doubt—inside she could see
too the impression of unimaginable
sunsets,
only happening out there—while we
we are not looking
but the tug goes still and the sky holds—
holds it to the blue pages—
to bring home to her.
like a rat. in a bow tie.
smiling at small beds to a family
of also cartoon rats, in bow ties
(imagine that!!!!)
if only in a gesture of the shoulders—
and a look—that something amazing
still stands
even if that wait meant.....
well......
just inside a man,
and if that man were the one—
the one under the blue lights—
and nightstars

pulled into the junk ship
a tug
binded
binded and the splinters went in
and i felt each one, and i am a tug
on this ocean of ours...

but
i am standing on this fucking beach.

CHAPTER 2

Smoking and Bug

so many years old
but
not a man
  at all
  am i
this weird place
so much
bedroom noise
radiator making clangs
this whole night
like a stretch
of beach
with blond and salty bangs
  or
candy cane missiles
projecting
light orbs over
blankets cursed under
backache
and
why did i stop or even start
  what

a
dumb
kid
i have been that for so long
pointless really
isn't it
to act like this
or that
say we get lost in a moment
say we get gone in the fly rods
casting
outward
to sea on expensive dinghies en masse
spanish armada omelets
diner fantasy food
outward upward
dreaming
half-assed and awake
i miss someone
so much
i quit
well, smoking
really
to prove to myself
how strong
a love is
even for me
so many years old

and not a man
  at all
  in years
but terribly
  terribly
overwhelmed by
  a name
and mercy
be a woman
with her name
and me
imagine this
not smoking
wowed
secret loud backwards lot centered
alive arms out
planted
in the new days

Hover

one click in my gear past this flimsy breath
i set this stone adrift
in the hover
on a movie set river
side
blasting cool wind
on my face here
  i imagine i am walking down SHOE AVENUE or 8th STREET
my word did i abandon you,
my cinderella nothing,
old me
"fantasy sizes" me
in the gusts of bought things
sold sale sell it all mind me—
we walked away together—
whore feet
whore boots
all on my tippy-toes not to alarm myself
and
there and there and here
all over
    New York City got behind me—like bad checks—so unlit

dimmer with each breath—i was afraid it would all go—
tumbling from my winter closet
it all did
in fact
i went into the nearest cave
and sorted my abilities witch,
wizard and magic slave soldier
put myself into that envelope
mailed myself away, rings and
fantasy sizes all in one folder
manila colored
and just said out loud
so i might get it now
grow up man
she loved me
still
so now
oaks riddle this line
owls riddle this rope
swinging to a boat
easily
peacefully
drifting
and i am clicking in the gear with a start
position and a breath
breaking the rocks in the orange juice quarry
and dreaming again
about horses

girls
  and
all that stuff i learn while i am down for the day
with
  new ideas about how to stay put
  while
everything goes rushing by in the dull mash
  me here
in the hover

Plus Dreams

okay so it goes like this—
word clutter, endless—
thankless pitiful days
are planted and ready
and we are a new winter
already
but blip clang zap go
machines at night and
most of the time i am not
as much sad
as i am just, well...ready
and
nothing goes as fast as
this
whatever this is
this
which comes with blurheart
and repeat fizzle-stutters
this
which holds me to the pen
and
words guide the fastening

of a bushel of new days
plus dreams

Our Hearts, Okay

okay throw this to the dogs
wet
with regret and dirtysome
okay
let them eat wet cake too
drenched icing bleached
from cloud, gray grotto
broke mirror lotto
machine-broke
dirty machine
actual grimy plastic bits
skycomedown
always looking
one light on arcade
kinda
okay
let the wet dogs then go into
new dream houses because
well
our hearts also heal
this is the new miracle
the miracle

is this

heal someone else and you get fixed

no shit

ok, anyway

so sorry but that's how i got the lights on

that's how the lights go on

and the parts get worked

and fixed and moving

and clean in this damn

machine

that thing

what is that thing anyway

it's that greasy metal wheel on a dusty flat desert plot

moving the red oil through

in the splintered sunlit growl

our hearts

moving together like machines

in the past

moving through time

in the ok corral

on stilts

smashing

rain wet

birthday cakes

ok

let's party

Papercut-Sunrays

quick come see
a radio tower leans forward
color spins
in the sequence of geography
living maps
unfold forward in green and autumnal red blocks
lined aside each
in their bands of gold
striped with rooftops
and
signs for fireworks and beer
no one ever really moves
away
move away now
by the windows in the battleship sky
with splinters of foggy growls beside
these are new days
new days
papercut-sunrays plus the neighborhood
it is painted with hope not dry rot
or molded stores
inside the mall

nope
these are new days
everything has been made of crystals stitched
in new quilted patches
smiling almost—not almost now—
just smiling—teeth out
in a riddle of us
inside this egg cracking slight
and with new meanings
these are new days
quick come see

No Mask

no mask
quiet loud
arms fall
side by side
then
silence
then
into dream
i go
upwards
inside
and
perfectly bound
like
i was a chosen thing
to be a chosen thing
is
also love
but
activated
and
like a storm

i get to be
floating by and thru
and
maybe
that means a me
and
maybe
that means a you
maybe
but for now
just
this
a divided line
and
so much direction
from
silent guides
my heart
is still
i keep it
it is mine
and
we are now kites
built out of glides
and
i can't wait to fall asleep again
and again
this time
wow

Fixtures Rot

in time the fixtures began to rot
one by one
off the wall
the wallpaper sunbleached
from missiles and house holes
suddenly but not so suddenly
one by one they grew forgot
as forgetful things go
they go this way
when the light recedes into
eventual fade
like father nodding off
in his thanksgiving sofa chair
football stove-top stuffing snore
beer or a television tray
noise from his nose
no on or off clickless
underneath the stairs
a box of remote controls
one for every year they made
bad tv's
upstairs in the dresser

in a shoe box tied with strawberry laces
a bundle a fistful
of imagined lockets
go rusted
with coins too
all that change unusable even now
even now
as the world changes
also
a list of names of our ghosts
first and last
i whisper them out
under my breath
like
endless beggings of our dogs
sweet names
and
chocolate paws
from a past
howl echoes
forgotten to a fog
and a wind
even now in fine steps
a silver string collects
new shatters
webbed patterns
underneath binders
of a long sigh

or
a collected regret
a color that remains
only of the name
a woman could ease into
and burn
into a single flame
mark
simple and in context
I between M and A
not in any order
held closely to the day
its low lights
a calendar of gauzy rays
swimming
so fast
in a near sea-blast
once perfectly safe
in a harbor of such calm
it is unknown
from any single day
any book or story
if it were a heart
so blue
from blackened lots
and wishing
so true
so

tortured and forgot
but in a time
in a time before the fixtures went rot
and the mirrors came down
let us back into that moment again
and we
we will never let it down
for its perfect lean
against two
all dreams
and
back to back
with perfect light
pink
reflecting no days fading
with two
sunken in
on skin

Ironing

the heat
on the bottom
binds new things
to old
like us

Goodbye, New York City

    goodbye i say
                goodbye youth, dad
goodbye big city
              and those stain
glass
    nightmares i used for pillows
the moon is in the icebox tonight
shit
no weather
no sound
nor wind nor clouds
no colors
no sunset nor sunrise
in the freezer all night freezing
shit
  pirate ships race across the carton of ice cream
and make little turbine engines and fires in tiny garbage cans
on the street in hobo garb it is always 1986 in the freezer dad
damnit or something someone screams up the alleyway over
moonlighting or thirtysomething or me crying loving the
punch
line

the moon is in the doghouse no steeple-chasing stunt
coordinator
can pull this old tin can back on track with the clouds no
more neon
without a reason right—gosh what a waste that whole city
that whole place
they built that place to be meaner than electric robotic
snakes still
everyone is dancing so disney and i mean maybe i cannot see
it that
far away from the drugs i just see the scowl and the false
colored nails
building tops
like hammer drops
on snares on cymbal flares
signal fires and crossed wires
FBI screeching tires on tv
and no me
i am in my sunset dream in my jammies
jamming on cooked summer squash and
james dean milkshakes no milk something
else please
                    and totally happy now that i know
what a ghost is if it is me
and me loving a city that
lost grip of the edge of its
own higher floors mid-dream
the suspense not waning the

film projector spools out and
flap flap flap goes that roll and
we see just the white and really
no one is left to boo this

                                  not me

not you

       i am in a canyon now in love
imagine that and for serious real with
total conviction i think
i know
now

   just

       when to say when,

                             goodbye youth
goodbye new york city

CHAPTER 3

New Gods

soft dreamers feathered like bird monsters
us folks fix cars; lean against old motors in
gray dawns smoking cigarettes—fresh out
of the dryer washed blue jeans and some
old fucking jacket;
didn't finish school—got gypped a grade—
too depressing
blue sparklers going off behind those dark
really too-thick-for-a-face glasses and so so
pretty for a loser;
i mean
america is spitting us out these boys/girls
america is making a new store for us haha
to work in—for
who will rob us when we are busy with the
customers?
i think it might be safe to say—with
red lipstick back of grandfather's car making
out—switchblade carrying—greased hair—or
those long legs and that gingham-checked
dress all fucked in the night sweat summer
fuss—all hot—gone to the pulped paperbacks

falling apart into dust
it's probably time
time to throw in the chips dad and
well
let in the new gods

Back to Us

we pass through these days like sunlight
through gauzy wet sheets
damp
and yellow in the backyard
riddled with hopeful light
and
my world is nothing but day
and
it was the silence stirring in the room
that sent
my dream
back
to me
and
back to you
or
back to us
always
back to us

Windows

it's nice to be away from all those mirrors
    8th street
    9th street
2nd avenue
    each building each wall
    another mirror
    another shadowfall
in the sidewalk
boots and cloaks
    and
new clothes
everywhere, pink carnations floral print
on bleached whale-skin sky
print blue and white
antique shop shoulders
    black camera eyes
    installed
always looking
back
    it's nice
    to be away
it's nice to be away from all those mirrors

        red witch
        ice witch
witch mountain
        every morning every moaning noise
        another haunting
        another curse withdrawn
in the bank buildings
they build a court
        and
new nets
to watch the checks bounce, purple uniforms
blur past the seats with the tv stars
sucking face into the vacuum of time
on the stove fried eggs burn
        kitchen smells like
        burnt onions
always looking
back
        it's nice
        nice to be away
        from all that

Full Tilt

bicyclemad
born dizzy
i am
flying off the cliff of panic hill
   umbrellaless
doing/doing/doing the twist
bicyclesick—
my broken spoke,
  my past;
    that angry kid throwing the stick
    into my tire from the curb—past
  wheelspinning
  bullygrinning
   me
   knees on fire
  handlebarjumping
  asphaltskidding
   past
what calms me down—in the ditch
   teethbusted blue
   in that ol' spin of mine
is a quiet

is a voice
is a note
is a flurry
white on white-polka-dot-alright-sheets of static
roar all day—roar all night
   in the khaki-lit room for one
between the letters of a hotel sign;
   red hot neon blue
now Full Tilt and so so
filled up...
      a room service staff waiter
      with a bowl of fish
      i am
      returning champagne glasses
      in the mail slot
down the mast of a wooden ship
a laundry shoot am i
i am
a junker bent from that cross gale
(maybe)
   southern bit-lip honey mouthed
tale spun
spun out
drawn out
overdrawn
sails up
junker bent
tense

ya know—in one slow movement
like an orchestra tuning and
then out of the silent woody
reeds
a hilly crest—a fallen army on that
hilly crest thing
or
a horizontal sunrise colorblast
blueberry naughty
and all
  "calm the fuck down"
engine purring
  in me
    nine lives
      plus three
        and a movie
in a rush to get home
            for good
this is what
it is
like
to wake
and hear my lover's voice

Sparklers

dreaming
this
　large meteor crashed into the
carwash—of my mind
　i am in the bed
ancient green blanket—
　dresses hanging on a wall—lots
lots of them, one over the other—
she is smiling
still naked
one week after—not even one week
and here i am
　　there i am
chinatown
a moment extractor or maybe
i am here to solder these two realities
together
with my tongue
　　what?
maybe i am yanking someone INTO
this
　　this is loud

ear hurts
dresses stacked up on a yellowish
accidental yellowish whitewall
with
cutouts
from magazines
  like anne's room
only
  flirtier
and
 wrong
full red colors yellow burst
haze
    it's just a voice
    a smile a kick—a heart stops
    goes better
these nights fading now
diners closing all around
murmuring shuddering
alone
and a kick back into the water
a man starts his way back into the sea
floating
swimming
    restarted
    unfrozen red meat
  bear
  i was born to stomp concrete

a subway was someplace nearby
or rattling by the bed something
went
CRASH under us
rusted grate by that bed—
neon blue
sky
    and cloud mass; electric eyes
outside—
    dirty air conditioner—behind
    my therapist sits on the moon
with his freudian books
and questions about mother
    he didn't understand
    my whole life
was a gesture
of appreciation for punk rock
    like a kicked-in bedroom wall
    or unwed mother baby
    party ready
    and
    clinic bound
we destroyed your generation
your world wars neighborhood bars
became radio signals
falling out of the apollo
like space junk
    and booze satellites

we keep our lovers
in our cell phones
under pseudonyms
justincase...
chinatown gets icy
so there
dreaming myself up
was i
perfect in that moment—perfect
chinese bells ringing also—also—
i am a visitor in this kingdom
always
yes
drunks outside were clamming up
for morning—a new showtime or
a series of flow and stop
breaking patterns
we digress
always
at the sheet parts
total wet kiss and
total wet shower
sparklers
on
yard is on fire
we call for help
with
mutual dreaming

and tears
a bear wanders out of the campsite
chewing as he smiled
   curbside
"bon voyage nutso"
   so long
chinatown
   my clumsy
   smiling plateau
nice
farewell shiny city
   my dreams
dreaming

Night Blooms Sweet

just there over that border neal said there is madness
i liked that
i am almost invisible then, almost always
cloaked
as it might be
as it were
in that madness—
   mexico
is right at the end of this street
with plastic neon color packages
stuff
hanging everywhere; junk; awesome
people
ancient faces—cars booming systems
easy sunblast into several alleys
the alleys are cleaner than the streets
it got dark
i went back into the shitty hotel
thought about smoking
how i quit
and all those amphetamines
quit those

it's like drifting
for nothing to do
but see and feel time's sluggish gait
night blooms sweet
like a pepper in a bowl
and el paso
wraps its fingers around the branch
and shakes the sky for its stars
and they fall
all around the parked cars
and
radio noise
i hear all that right now
in this room
someplace out the window

Nonsmoking Dream

water-skiing in a cosmic void
baby
now THAT
is a nonsmoking dream

    also

hot librarians doing stuff in
knee-high socks
THAT
      is none of my business
but
   i figured i'd sell somebody
something
       secret
why
   not

Snowflakes, Curtains, and All

with the same force as a snowflake hitting the windshield of
a parked cop car
on the abandoned frozen awful avenue
her lips crash into my eyes
quick as a flash of lightning
steeple-bound
and the house comes down
so to speak
and those people who are not there in that opera house of
pitchy penguins
all stand and r o a r endless roars tiger mouth roars lion
tears loud hunt like
and
i know i have to leave that city for good
whatever a goodness demands and the thing is
she loved it because i could spice it up still
i can most things
i talk around the flaws
but this place i lived
this crystal wall of what
it is not going to stop breaking long enough that i can reflect
that dim light

back onto its interiors and let it free so to speak
and i loved it so
how i loved it
but
with the same exactitude as a mountain lion falling into the
tar pit foolishly
and with branches inside to save him placed ironically
her shoulders ease and slump beside me
fell like delaminating beach furniture
white streak riddled cute yellow
we fall even harder
and the house comes down
so to speak
in one big gigantic thud
curtains and all
ha}

Now I Sing My Life

"now
i sing
my life
for you
i will not be leaving
going
anywhere anymore without you
i am in a place
now
in here
totally growing
whether it be me in one place
you at my heart quick
never slowing
like a thumping putter
like my own skin feels a sun or moon reflecting a sun
sunshining breezeblowing
or
beside you steady
steady or not
hand firmly in yours yours in mine
together

and
like here we come really
willing to forgo all that mindful heavy-heartedness
for a smile and a breath
because
well
you make me feel like smiling
me not knowing
and
you make me feel loved
like it was the first time
and
it truly is
truly mindblowing yes
you were the key that broke the seal
if my soul were locked
now
i sing
my life
for you
my love"

Go I

go i
go ahead into your arms
dizzying spun back
crystal soul
you
so swallowed by this moment
that is what i am
and will be
sleepless (always)
or
faint or too left out to wait
see,
i waited my whole life for you
you
dizzying spun back
mouth lifted to the sun
to drink in the day
my feet ache
to follow you more
to
hold your hand like i was nothing
and

kind of everything from go again
see,
real love restarts a man
restarts a man's heart and
soul
if he lets it
you
you are there waiting at the gate
where the flags wave
in the afternoon breeze
and
they are all lined up nose to nose
and
fresh-cut grass glimmers on each side
my feet ache
i am running so fast
to you
engine running
heart puttering
words stuttering
forward
into these miracles you call moments
where
our eyes meet and noses touch
and
i race a new day to the quick
for your hand
and

for your laughter
dizzying spun back
go ahead into your arms
go i

CHAPTER 4

Future/Past

brace yourself
here is the ending
it starts with a bang
and descends
through a patch of
briarcloud and mash
pulp
hard lines driven
the center to circle side
of your face
so new each time
my mind erased
the last sketch—
and even in that
that darkness—a
new thing
a new thing happens
and we got lost
in the blast—we/us
in a future/past

FutureFucked

outside the dreariness of a poor dream i go inside myself for
luck.
why,
well
a bee landed in my coffee and i guess i turned it on its head
i was afraid i might win
again
that ticket you reclaim nothing
you hand in your pride
like an i.d. you show
to get into a bar
i don't go to bars
my body is a prison already
why drown it
so that it's like i am hiding even further
even further in the back of the cell
behind the blanket
green and wool
and
futurefucked.

What a Bad Idea

what a bad idea
that was
   that i wanted to haunt myself
   i did. period
   that i wanted to even it up—?
   i did. comma
see—
that was
   me
   on the pretend
   me
   on the typewriter
   me
   on me, all over me
   me
   using the worst i had
   for more
what a bad idea
that was
   that i wanted to shake myself
   i did. shook
   that i wanted to steal thunder—

i did. thunderstruck
see—
that was
   me
   on the way here
   me
   showing myself ghosts
   me
   inviting the bad stuff in
   me
   soaking up the floor with the fear
i collected
   like i had a cold in my heart
this
     is
       sneezing
     not
kinda
   on the mend
i had to let it out
to get well
   what a bad idea
   that was
but i did
   i did
   i did
that was
   me

Me and Joan of Arc

me and
joan of arc
at a television station
i asked her if she wanted to go to the beach
she said no way
and
i was really really sick
i mean
supersick; like—awful in the head
still
we like it when we get pretty words
stuck to the roof of our mouths
like dogs
with peanut butter mouths
and someone over us
pretending we are talking
as we move our jaws
in time
to the jibber-jabber
doing ape splits over jump ropes
etc.
and i needed to go to the beach

or anywhere

and

she needed to say no again

and

again and again

at the television place

other people i knew well were also

there and they looked like

they had seen me crazy

so many times

so much

that

if i was upset so what, so what

so what

joan is allowed to go fighting into the sunset with the brave

swordsmen

bloody feet and all

so i took her black lipstick and wrote a note for the angry

mob

on a call sheet

and i stapled it to the stake

we laughed

as some smartass in the crowd turned to his buddy, derrick

and punched him in the shoulder

and said

"burrrrrnnnn"

and snapped his fingers

like a split second later

like a drag queen would've
black and white days lasted forever
i loved me some black and white days
and
black and white nights
in the black and white city
still
it was all pain
there i was
again
at the television station
me and
joan of arc
no beach
not that it mattered
i paid for a holiday there
i just never went
i don't even like the beach
and
that was that
now i am here—in the sunlight
undertow
ready for the colorized prime time
no war
new president
sober
golden
now

drumroll please
quietly kind of
happy

A Colorful Ending

a book of poems
by me
everyone so happy celebratory
before reading
party ready and smiling teeth confetti
totally upsetting
  i know, i know
  alright already
  me
  cut it out
without the music all those words, they're not so funny
not true
not kind
not me
but there they are
there they are—across the page
up and down like a depressive
box of chocolates
one second an elevator
the next a cage
with amphetamines and xanax
inside as slaves

to that guilty planet i walk alone
in its frozen wintry tundra
ice-cream cold
with ice-blue bowling ball eyes
inside i am screaming but outside i am calm
all "what?" and like "did that happen?"
course not
but alone biting the pillow
walking the halls like a ghost
in a perpetual self-haunt
i wrote what?
i didn't even know i was on drugs
till i saw the ink stains on my paws
howling with sleigh bells
takeout vietnamese food
crazy like a fox
hungry like a dog
my face licked clean with a skull tongue
inside the house
the horror so clear
so blue
it broke open that sky
it rained waterfall pills
my umbrella mouth
sponged
all the sadness
into a single cracked taco shell
brain dead

and staring into the antenna on the apartment wall
through the back windows
on the corner of my bed
smoking my last cigarette
over and over
over
and through
out came a me
and
out came a you
out came us
into the caves we went
clock and dagger—
shadow and light bearer
servant on servant
master on master
   cloud-hunting on our sides, our backs grassed
   sky wincing in golden sunrays
   the beach lined with firefly twinkle little star
   lights on lights on blur pools
the bright monumental expressive gusts
of your voice
eruptions of laughter and total disgust
i trust you with the treasure of my secret soul
imperfect and tired like a mountain of burning tires
   your kisses strawberry shortcake ridiculous
   asking "what do you think" and "when do you think"
   blah blah blah blah blah

knees weak—composition rubbed round the edges

total cliché and bedridden

slowing down

not escaping

decadence dependency almost gone—

like a shot of dope—memory smeared and

vodka mind erasers mind erasing

me into a little stop

the past has grown weak

and elderly-couple loud

clumsy and cute

destitute and proud

the future's glasses grown fogged

patches of fruit growing up through the cracks

in the walk

out back

that fucking book i wrote for ten years

on drugs

just another doorstop

to drool on

once i let the hopeless shell break

and i get confused for somebody's dad

words broken on the stove cooking gas

smoke

like an old man

like a caboose stunt gone wrong

i wrote

i walked fingers on keys like legs on wooden planks

between the steel and rusted tracks
my timing in the steel yard
clicking along with the clock
for kicks
and for a year's notice
that calendar all ours
all mine
   that sun rises on the in-between
   on the subway marching bald heads bodies
   on jackets and shopping trolleys
   avenue thieves, snotty flu children
   on the brother waiting in the station
   for his friend
   who has never seen his face grown old
   and never will again
   once the crows call and walls break
   in the tornado shake back home
my past is out for the lamb
i am the shepherd
it won't shake
its bloodhound nose
sniffing at me in the bushes
round the lake
   my words
   my my, my word
   little army of battle-ready soldiers on horses
   tiny arrows
   adding up

to bring the elephant down
so pink
frozen in the corner with airplane glue
and sniffing sneezing
glue-heads
laughing
like a cackle-box got born again
on a television
stroking my hair
this moment turns me on my back
like a tortoise
because
i pulled ghosts from the fishing pool
in my mind
    and
you can tell that story
    and
like everything i did
i put it up for sale
but old me,
    goddamn man
    you're so sturdy
just how funny is it now
what i became
so far back here
is just how far
and how loud
you fell

my words, your words
that scrambled past
heartbroken
buried on the moon
still alive
frozen in time
i know, i know
alright already
but
you are lucky to be alive
for the times i tried to end you
plus countless prayers
for
some colorful ending

Flight Pattern

i ascend
up a continental bend
missed you
somehow
up into the rafters of baked clouds
and passengers
before i could beg
beg for a new day's word
i ascend
now into the city
knowing
i will only sit in that room forever
and sleep if i can
like a fool
waiting
stuck mindlessly in a solid
unchanging
flight pattern
where we do not cross
which
as always
is my loss

Poets Smoke

poets smoke
they issue cool in a flick of dashed lines
collar bolted shut by the button
smoke from the fingers
shoulders slouched arched
puff
lips parted no words long stare
words in their marbles
spinning in place
eyeball plates
that was me
trying
poets smoke
now
i am so really screwed
i am not smoking
damnit
here i am all set free—buildingless
spires cooled and on the walls around me
the eyes of the dagger
the pen loaded
like a bullfighter's halo crimson and ghost coming church

burned red

damnit

i got set free

every time i see the inhale i see the cancer ripping apart the
lungs

i see war drums and toxic marsh lands and zombies

ripping through all that helpless pink flesh

them lungs ripped by the smog monster

that stick of "fuck you and go-fuck-yourself-myself-my body"
yelling

yelling that through blood raining down on

the emphysema-riddled dawn

the street concrete gray blue neon-blue sky

one white cloud

and in the alley

milk cartons and cigarette butts litter the brick surrounding
each side

like it rained candy paper

in there the ghosts of the wars my grandfather fought are in
there with him

he is dying again

on the oxygen machine

crying

for his life

he was losing

because of the arch-shouldered-poet smoking trick

because of what the twenty years did

did for me

because when it hits your lungs you just kill it some more
each time
plus coffee in the morning and somehow
somehow it's okay
but
what if it killed your wife too because it lingered in the halls
of the house
and who you were built to protect
you kept out the rats
the mice
the serial killers
the poison vats of crack
and
instead
you let in the fog that caused sixty types of cancer immediately
no matter what
and
she dies alone after you die because you hit that arched
golden door
poets smoke harder
what
for?
for a reason to have the suit match the insides of the
    darkened palace
of bad posture
and reckoning
i think not
i got set free

thank god
i got set free
one more day alive
uncool
breathing in the elmed-car-lined neighborhood air
while
poets smoke

The Bible Sold Lots, Didn't It?

ooops

who wrote that one

not me

pill mountains and

scary me did

i just wanted to build something huge

instead i built something scary

  and tall

and the only thing that tore it down

was showing it to somebody

   anger and all

fucked eyes

L M N O P damnit

now i am something i can live inside

instead of me

living inside me

like i was a city

or a growing thing on those pills

pill trees

   raining down click clack heart attack patter feet

then

   slow slow slow slow slow slowing down into the

cold feet bed

man

what the cat ate killed all kinds of ideas

about grace

not a parakeet named that either

but

    a face

i think about my turning the wheel

this red car past the store we are in now

this life

flier

wow

and i go, all southern inside voice

"i got a copilot

a woman

all the time,

i kiss her bottom lip when she joke smiles

lying there in the forever nook

unafraid of love all of a sudden

and i am all like

let's fly this thing together—"

    a face

bigger than my problem mountains

than my city i rung up

from the front desk of the settled-down masted

ship and

i sang all loud like a drunk warbling in tennis shoes

and shorts and shiny beads

honda-ready burbling
   i wrote this book and it was just scary
the kid says "it's giving me nightmares"
and i know
   it won't matter
   until he gets a headache
bigger than that
and
   maybe he might
build something
now
   out of disappointment
fingers crossed
the bible sold lots, didn't it
and
who wrote that one

Repeat

etc.

repeat

repeat

repeat

Rock gets covered by paper, right?

Scissors cut paper, right? How many

fingers is that one?

Mirror reflects light catches paper

on fire, right?

How many fingers is that

if

the words inside said

"Rock gets covered by paper, right?

Scissors cut paper, right? How many

fingers is that one?

Mirror reflects light catches paper

on fire, right?

How many fingers is that

if

the words inside said"

repeat

repeat

repeat

etc.

Our Dreams Went South

our dreams went south
big kid
silent to the melody
again
the sound
of our dreams
and
to the words

a test drum pattern lands on his nose
this butterfly bum
er,
me
and all i know is
all i know is that
       maybe
maybe from the mouth down
maybe
maybe that was supposed to be you
  wearing those curtain rod–yellow rose of texas scarfs
  and
  muttering to yourself like you were your own lover

half drunk
    only a cruel bastard would laugh
    i just stare
but
  from the mouth down—all loud CRACK BANG
  forgetting the arc and the swing
  forgetting
  the
  wrist
    a lover's movement
    like stroking the hair from a neck
    all naked and bent
  CRASH THUD
  music notes fall from a scale
  ears bleed
  radios yuck out
and your word
saying all that
high-end bells
     and
hijacked and
all of a suddened
but
pah rum pah pum pum
goes that thud and
    crack
and
all i hear is

that sound
like a beaten man's door slam
all the way to the broke bank
and music
not so much
not so much
    but you will always say it was me
    who worked it like a working girl would
    who couldn't stand it alone
    I held the bastards back
    at the gate
    leaving myself hostage
while you stood with your finger in your mouth
staring blankly into the surf
like you were born
into helpless children
forever faceless and forever slow
    and
that is totally why i left
our submarine so empty of dreams
i slept
to the words
and you stood helpless
to the sounds
      because
you were never really listening
in the first place
so much night

music missing
    in the light
underneath us and lights-out
and
our dreams went silent
and
our dreams went south

Help

help i think i went HELP skin was screaming
skin, my skin was SCREAMING something
rashes and welts
and
bad bad gas
awful
simply, i was going through some kind of hell
i am so serious
so so
serious
all this and an alley cat and christmas is coming
christmas is coming
ah fuck

ah fuck
i was sitting on the airplane and i knew something
was funny my hands are numb
fever broke
and
now i know it is cold
although my chest still hurts and my stomach it is hurt bad
maybe got holes in it

chest might got holes in it
ear canals have holes in them,
i can't hear, breathe all that well or welt well
i don't welt well
i panic
and
i am far too vain
vanity becomes me like you have no idea, seriously
just a bastard inside, i am, about all that
am i dressing it too down
am i
i always dress down
i am too beautiful for you.
help.
so help,
right?
haha
no way.
no fucking way can you,
can you?
haha
help.
you fall for that one every time.

White Diamond

Lots of things make noise,
even nights
can make all that noise
so i stopped building noise factories inside my house
typing away into the void,
   into the hurricanes

i stopped
building yapping machines out of strangers
and letting in the gas from the dream cemetery
swamps
that noise sounded funny
then bad
like a scream for help
if it was helpless fast
so i quit
   into the hurricane

i stopped looking at those ghost pictures and
i stopped listening to those disembodied voices
   with
     so many opinions

that almost

for how cruel and negative

a person can be

they forget to have their own...

you know, identity

so easy these people are

nowadays like dominoes falling into place

when someone starts the smear campaign

yelling "come on" engines starting

people so easy—with words

these blind fools word marching

burning torches with words

out their bedrooms

out their back rooms

he starts the dogs

gnarling gnashing teeth out the gates

it meant nothing to read books

or

to capture summertime things in your hand

or, well

...kisses

those "sloppy fucking hand up your skirt"—

...kisses "running fingers across the side of your back

down to where you arms fold then...stop"—...kisses...

nope

the word marches roll through the word towns of

museums

the night watchman is beaten down with words

while
the night watchman is sleeping—and the paintings
come down
burning one by one
to the ground
on a pile with the other artifacts and the folklore
and
whatever wasn't bolted to the ground
even the ink pens in the bank with the chains
they were swinging empty on the bottom
over the wood-paneled counter
if they were an idea
you could race the others to the yard with
and stand there on the banks
of the cliff
and
with all that music
watch it go over the side of the quarry
   and fall
like a classic car
exploding on the rocks
everyone standing there
at their keyboards
   blank
like a killer's
eyes
   it's super weird
people have stopped counting

on their hands
and
in their heads
   everyone is ON SOMETHING
   in their mouths twice a day
   or ON SOMETHING
   electric bicycles
   staring blankly into screens
   and
   those screens have funny lines going across them
   when you videotape them—
   and people look like they are in a trance
disappeared and
so sad
at the end of the entrance
with no-exit blank eyes
and carrying it now nervous
their little palms always stuck
to their faces
with their devices
unaware of how pretty
it is to be out walking
in all these amazing places
riddled with billboards
screaming into the alleyways
like glass floating houses
   into the hurricane
   oh well

i pretend i am a hovering diner
full of fucked pirates in their oil-stained linen shirts
cuffs out
smoking and being asses, beer-gutted and crook-toothed
and/or
i am surrounded
in a white formica silver-and-gold flecked booth by
library anomalies
the diner is me but a robot me with shiny insides—
silver on the walls
    real metal
in the back—where the swinging doors swing
when the BELL pops and goes RING
like a cat
moving moving across porcelain pizza boxes
reading minds like a psychic trucker
his hand twitches and reaches for the coffee scalding
    hot,
always,
as dawn fades up and down like it is note guessing
the bridge
in a trap
called
...get this...
"the white diamond"
the old lady summer waits it out till the heat dies and
it's always someone else's fault
isn't it when it changes so slow and

with one flash of the bulb—swish
that picture is made
and
it's your fault
if you kept
reading
the menu
    your name was always right here in the back
next to mine
because
    we always loved each other so so much,
    stranger
we always loved each other this much before the
screens went on
before the mystery was undone
and we forgot our telephone digits by heart
our addresses not places on a street
or
halfway up a building side overlooking the highway
but things we typed into the beast
the beast
inside us an insecurity and a nagging pang
forever hungry

San Pedro Park Blues

this dog started following me
he looked scary
it was only a few minutes maybe
maybe
after the taxi let me off
in this tennis school/school yard
in the middle of a hot texas fucking day
that i knew
ah fuck
no skateboard park here
and
there was this dog
thinking i was his owner
or
i was going to be easy to eat
he looked like a wolf
i remembered
what a neighborhood was
and
was fucked for a ride
because
people don't take all that many taxis in texas

and
in san pedro park
you just walk home
i guess
that poor wolf dog

CHAPTER 5

Saturday

"Like it isn't real i get this palm on my neck
fingers moving
so sweet
like it isn't saturday i am lost talking/listening
man
palms spinning sunlight sparklers behind my eyes
up there in my brains in my brains dreaming
midday
god
i really like you i really always liked you
and
whatever this is
thank god
i surrender
let the light in all the way and bury it all
under the yellow lift of hope
take it
take all that bullshit all that madness all that rocked-senseless
sadness
take it back now before it's too late, whoever left it
 someone turned the lights on in here
in me

and i cannot see through the warmth
of the shield
of joyful ringing
mashed up like clouds like gamma
and
happy dumb and lifted
man
god
whoa
so so so
yellow sunned this winter
saturday
what a joyful blast of teeth and well
just
just thanks
i always liked you so much,
you summertime
you smiling
but this
this is different
this is
forget about it
and
well like it isn't real
for that turning of the wheel
in my direction
blueblond neon hue
i am yours

and
i like saturdays
all over
all over again
fuck yeah"

Super Good/Keep Looking

supergood
    keep looking
hi
    turns out my love, true
    is not a concrete lot
sans auto
nice graffiti
big yellow words—bloomed
each letter all curved
mellow and laughing
almost
bent round a sunlit
kiss
  nope
    turns out my love, true
    is not a twisted branch
tree floating
on a hanging
island
like above clouds—moving
in slow hover rhythms
  nope

             i like how this all happened
             to me without the thinking
             something came in here
             turned the house (my soul)
             its parts
             upside down
like a big old party happened
inside my face
          ha
with the umbrella outside
upside down
catching next-day light
          and
some of that morning stuff
bending the books back
in a page
   nope
             i like how this all happened
turns out my love, true
has no edge
bends like a
smiling burrito
wedge of ice
or glass faces
all blinking
disco grits in
synchronicity
plus

or minus
bragging rights
there is a god
and
it is up to something
supergood
keep looking
keep looking

Smiling Like I Was New

Smiling like I was new
I sat there
full of fish bones and a tanker of panic
I was your summer nightmare
with some tail wagging
and
a happy ending
somewhere
and I stank of bad decisions
and, well
you loved me
and I knew when I knew that it was true
that the ride was soon over
that hell ride I grew comfortable in
and now
now here we are,
here I am—
my love—
see...
Those ghosts and I
we aren't talking
for good

not since I drafted myself
into this army of the living
this battle for the days
hands clean
the only blood loose
running through my veins
heart on fire
gnashing clichés
I say
"I am closing this cemetery,"
what?
did I stutter, no
nobody is laughing
eat my dust
I left
throwing my hand to the air to catch the bar
bar assembled left and right
attached firmly to the wheel
wheel spinning against the sky
I closed that lot of gone
bogging it with a brick as if it were a hole
For Once,
the sea rings its bells on this blast of beach
in my mind, where the tide goes
its gusts long
and
tampered with by mischievous drafts
this house of spirits

this place of holy or sacred love
this new beginning I mistrusted
no,
you may not have it
this is mine
but
if you must
go forward and find this in yourself
because
when I said there is no hope
those words,
they betrayed a faith or else why say it,
I was wrong too
no,
those ghosts and I,
we aren't talking
and
I am closing this cemetery in me
for good
because
I broke my porcelain baby doll head
erupted
floor dropped from speeding arms
doll like heads
on this thing in me
stubborn
in love
riddled with faith
smiling like I was new

Whale Ships

glorious sun
my imagination is an entire city under siege
it is under the control of my doomed snickering will
my crooked laugh
ah fuck
you could win the whole thing if you broke my nose
if you broke my spell, my heart, my mayflower
my liberty bell
my spanish armada
now our memories are turning orange-brown
like backyard nighttime cricket sounds
   under the pools of light on elm street
   breeze slow
or our youth
   capsized debris boxes of treasures wine bottles or clothes
   or candles
washing ashore onto the jagged rocks lining the coast
thunderstorms moving far off on the blurry horizon line
we were totally free
drugs fucking money
how in the world
did we complain

all that cocaine
talk
words like snake-sailors
coasting in the waves, between the rocks
our fleets
anchored there waiting to take us
now once again to war
gunpowder hands
into the deep with the ships
with the pirate battalions
off the coast
off the beach
cannons sending blasts everywhere
ducking the explosions and bird-scatter
i was on this life raft, it was my home
for words
i am an author laughable
for luck
i loved you and those things so very very much
the raft skipping like a pond rock on tiny surf
just off this coast,
just off the sidewalk
it cannot take us back to drug wartime
or depression
and takeout on the bed between fits of easy madness
i was a king
once
so unaware and so beautifully perched there—

on the scale

over a pit of fire

burning a fuel made of youth

my my

now,

on the beach, lover

one rush and dash for the sandhills up the beach

those daylilies seagrass breeze and sky

they burn bright

under the bullet-spray hair standing up on end

the mad dash saves us

and

the enemy above in smoking sniper towers familiar

the old us

holds true in our bloody dreams in the suburban hush

my past

those nightmares between movies

blockbuster black

the funny ones

the big ones

the ones you see on tuesday night

when it isn't busy

counting the years by things that go by us

too fast

like we were

i lost you

and us

and it

whale ships firing harpoons into the huddled mob of
blue mist
crying amazing tears
young
and
free
that war not claiming me
so hurt
continuing without the fade
or purple heart charade
my age dissolving me into nothings
cussing
us on a bed complaining
maybe you saw me age
maybe you saw me go tiger
and you go cage
so you bent the wires in your wiry frame
broadway litter scraping the tar
in swirling patterns between cars
like it was spelling your name
like it was on fire
like it was in flames
smoke circles bobbing from my mouth
in the freezing street
lottery-winning postures
no tomorrows—
all gone
totally wasted

evaporated
  home team away, forever
i cried like a fool
afraid of the new days
so scared
my youth on the stretcher
dying like a day
thoughtless motions arms in the air
in a ceremony unfit for prayer
but holy all the same
our shadows in the snowy landscapes in the shadows of
  macy's
and faceless alleyways
  the war
  big red cannons and the blast of victory
  claiming only a past life
  mortar falling debris around us
  one last time
that gray water falls safely on coral spears
a sea of whatever, some static
maybe
little rafts waving arms from little windows
some little spaces between squares colored
orange-brown, a tree between roads
no cars
places to hide myself in plus inside things set down
in the shattered landscape
comings and goings to and from this house

the animals sigh and lie down in the dust
where the grass was
ready for a summer's nap
that ocean quiets and one by one
those ships
they're going to get going
on its blue grill
   the war
   tiny destructions still lit in the ash
new and old
i am an arbitrator between
myself coasting into me, and water
the one clearing the vessels
perhaps
off this dirty beach inside my mind
where i let the whale ships rust or rot
going off to sea now
going into the bluish bull-pile
on that thing
what is it
our tomorrows,
our forevers
taking eternal steps each tearful exhausted foot
   like a hostage
   quietly
   without a sound
   smaller
   and

smaller
all the way
down
to
a
dot
.

Drift

we grow so old
right here
  so old,
  oh baby...
like seawebs or drifting power lines
hurricane bent
into my favorite lurch
  i miss you
while you are next to me
beached we are
in the blur of blue
    light
    ray
television slumbered we are not watching
we just like to be together
  under this
  canopy
  of safe
while...
while that world outside freezes
when we are together
it freezes

and

well

like a seaweb or drifting power lines hurricane bent

into my favorite lurch

   it drifts

   or

we drift

   with it

   clothesline—animals in the clothes on the clothesline—

plus everything

blurred colorful colored sunlit

   framing the whole lines of blowing clothes—blues jeans—

in the air—

saltwater air

booze breath

   oh shit

we grow so old

right here

   so old,

   oh baby...

Moon

So Moon...
you seem distant
dull even
lifeless
but
so much projection around you
so much projected onto you
the sun, for one
all up in your business at night
it is so hard for you to hide
and
you wallflower satellite
so many sing songs for you
in your name
you are unmoved
you neither like
nor dislike
it
the attention
you feel distant and you hover in place
if this were the prom
you would be back arched onto the gymnasium wall

watching the others dance
indifferent
but
you also feel no pressure
even though
the sea it relies on you to know when to give and take
itself to the land
its tide entirely up to you
you don't remember how
you don't remember when
the sea gave you that power
you don't care
back up against the wall
band playing a slow dance number
lipstick smeared on every other shoulder
moon,
wow
they love you down here
but
you don't care
you're so cool
moon
so cool

Good Things Too

   the litter of stars cuddle gaseous clouds
gamma and spitfire asteroid dust too
split like milkshake kids
running down an alley
like
the moon breaks a new cap on a can
of starlight suds
what?
exactly...
   this sky is blinking a flirty lash and beams
it just got back from the grocery store, smiling
new particles to add to the table of contents
in some lunar book
written in wishes
scribbled
those sky bags are full of names of people down here
on knees next to a bed or just sitting in the sunshine
in the park, or feet dangling over the side of the reservoir
in the summer mosquito swat midweeks—baseball game
seasons
you know
   the nighttime flinches or moves its muscles

its face, that vast dark, changing in the light
and all that stuff
we can't see
not so scary now
that the sheets are pulled tight over us
here in the safehouse bed
next to our loved ones
free from the boredom
of youngin questions
and
all that doubt
   those stars are twinkle-whats and shining lamps
for now which
by any watch
is longer than a hot minute
away from the pang
where the furnaces heat up the room
too heavy
for a panic
   i look up now for just me and anyone else in case
you know
   they need it
good things too
good things also need passing on

Artificial Lights

in a single solemn light
aside the drift
of the parachute lift
a song goes crashing
through my chapel roof
in the streets
the old lady sings too
her red handkerchief waving
at the tanks—lined with roses
on roped swings
dashing from the cannon mast
bellowing dogs and blond
girls in green military flank
jackets wave to the greasy GIs
and
from the roof
the constellations are all set fire
in the perfect grid and aligned
like it was christmas
in the television set
and
snowing on the model trains

moving through the motionless
little city
names, like jerry, john and moses
stationed somewhere post-stamped
and ready too, their faces were rubbed
newsprint charcoal until today
their lovers' eyes picking out the
wedding presents and their sisters
following their legs down the side
with imaginary thread, making perfect
imaginary dresses—
hands touching
all frayed knuckles and manners really
soda-pop corner store eventual crossed
fingers—before the car reaches the top
of the hill overlooking the city and
all those artificial lights
a new baby is born
in one quick sudden smile
it never rains here
anymore

Why Not?

just there

in the restless rush of eye-batting and lashings from

lashes smashing

below

those eyes

i see entire universes born

why not?

i see construction sites glowing with disco fires

why not?

i see my wife or maybe i see myself a husband

because

i was not married

not yet

anyway

just there

in the mashed potato salad marsh, or mush-mouthed

dog-eared days

gone by

your hands

they fold me into my time

so easy

i go without thinking into a single moment all born

now

so easy

i am here i can breathe heave faint last season's haints
fuckem
why not?
i see this woman i love so easily standing there
saying my name
smiling
just there
can you see her?
can you see your lover?
just there?
why not?

Yes

believe me
how strong a desire is
   yes
beaten wings go
in the sheetmounds
your lover does this also
   even if
you do not have one
in the bookstore
you see her legs her mimicked words
   putter
   putter
pitterpatter like water on a dry sink
   skinperfect
yes
   get it all over yourself
believe me
how strong a will is
collapsed neon sign
burst in the heatswells
greenlight redlight
greenlights

going gone
you do not have time
to stop yourself
  whisper
  whisper
name exchange and willow branch breaks
  all over
yes

Before That...

"...before that
before any lit
bellsrung and
the room goes
shhhhhhhhhhh
   i see
cottonsoft moments
replayed like time—
machines on projectors
and my heart goes cross
like something broken
from rain and rust
a bicycle reflector
or mirrored radioscope
deflector turned x vector
blasting whitesun midday
to catch gamma rays
of starlit wonders, like
well...
you
you...
in the longest best laugh ever

and the driving even starts to
go funny
...before that
i knew
how that might, just might, be the brightest thing i ever saw
in a smile with eyes
to match"

CHAPTER 6

California Forever

these fires within me are true
as her name is
seagulls spit fire over orange rind beach
again
ferry whalers tugboat oil tankers line up
like crooks
weekday simple light no forecast nothing
outside cool
winds blow soft like secrets zebra-striped
black-and-white
this is all inside me now in my heart as
i cross another ocean
it is summer here and it is also summer in
california forever
i am at the bottom of the world in terms of
how maps look
and future love binds me fast and quick to this
book of future spells
her name rings inside me like a cleaning cloth
over fogged glasses
that would be my insides answering up to the cook
deep at work

within me catching up on the nourishing and
these fires within me are true
as her name is
say it
over and over
this winter is binding itself to the rocks i cast my rod
out into the sea
this channel is stuck now
like for an eternity
on
california forever
whatever number that is
on a dial
as her name is
true
these fires within me
they are
as her name is

Hellosunshine

i love her
nobody never called me that
wakes me up every day and says
good morning sunshine
   i am blushing hard
   it splinters my cherry face
   all teeth
   eyes squinting
i love her
   my bug
she knows and there is that light again
the stairs inside our house are dim and
just cozy really
our love is an old house
minus drafts and plenty
of warm food and quilts
   my bug
she is out
climbing all these mountains, smiling, the mountains
they are breathless
truly
me too mister mountains

but because they see inside her we see inside the angel

because she does not

know how not to be true

she does not know a lie

  my bug

knows that feeling where you put your face in cold

ice water after the longest walk, neighbors waving in from

the heat, in from the cold

she is one of those hillsides riddled with yellow-white

fences

stained with hellosunshine and dirty wheels

like an american flag some salute

she is primary colors easy to understand

and represents too much for one person's

explanation

but everyone will try i bet once at least

if they stood around while she asked you

something easy and sweet

and

actually wanted to know

  my bug

a bowling alley cat like skeleton too much america but

all shining hard on the yard imagine the yard had plenty

of tomato vines and radishes in the ground

kitchen smells like cookies and candles and

cold milk but for the neighbors

smiling

rock formations inside me crumble when kissed

by her
i am always seconds from the dash in her name
the stroke of each letter, her day to me
is the times and i read the lines and
i don't ask all the questions i want
like a good book i hesitate before the ending
because
i never want this to end
  my bug
an easy everything to live inside and something
something shining and
that first glistening hope
that
now i believe in everything again
from go
  my bug
wakes me up every day and says
good morning sunshine
nobody never called me that
i love her

Hi,

hi,
a false ending gave us to each other
that ending, a letting go
time letting that end
have none of it
it gave me to you,
it gave these words to us,
you and me
and
we are now both still here
even if just in this very moment
where
something let us have it
whatever
this universal sweetness is
and
knowing that,
that
is what saved my life
if only
if only to tell you now
how much

how much
wishes mean
and
how very lucky we both are,
hi

You're Sleeping Now, Yes?

you're sleeping now, yes
yes, i can tell
i can see it when you are falling soon asleep you get lost
in almost breaths
and i pull strands from your forehead
kissing it
and think of peaceful peach waves of light
interrupting
inside i feel destroyed waiting to be rebuilt
like a ruin
in afternoon light
and
someplace nearby the whispers of figures
of us
shadowed with new tools
hover
and i love you
so much
yes
yes, you are sleeping now
and
god would be watching you if he existed or not

for
all that light

Bright as Stars

bright stars, geographical and located
inserted on oldish paper wrecked chalklike
letters and indentations
on a globe
with just outlines for land
and
black for oceans
THIS is some kind of freedom
and
how anyone would see it
on their way in
for the first time
right now
she is in the yard with the dog, the dog
has so many nicknames that one for every day
is more than one week
and a face
like grover from morning tv so sweet
out in the night shadows under palms
i can hear them laughing
both
in the cool pitch of mash dark shade

afternoon fade

her voice is a perfect pitch of lilting stemmed

somethings

pink and without end

bright as stars

we are

as we fall fast fast fast

asleep

Like This, Us

"us"
like this
us
just like this
hey
did you know
i cast out
this rod
so vast
so clean
it broke my name
over this water crest
and
sea-spray colored
if the sun heated it
until it went
tangerine
and
your smile
is that same color
it breaks my name
from the deep

releases me
from
bad checks
no sleep
any storm
spinning
rung out
till it is not a mole
on a mound
round a little creek
you
make
it
all
easy
love
or
you make it float
not-sinking
now
when i say yours
it is like the sky
whip-cracked a snap
like a cloud-split
or
everything with lungs
started laughing
even us

even us
even me
for
i have not felt this peace
before
like this love is
like this
us

Lucky

right here in the frozen clip
of this city
and everything before and after it
i sit
nothing but a tremendous yours
lucky
right here in the blundering white
of shift clouds
and cotton mountains of ice breath
i walk
nothing but a tremendous yours
charmed
over there in the sun-drenched west
my last home
where calm is stirred by gusts of smiles
i'm loved
nothing but a gigantic heart
shines
over there in your arms fit for a nap
born so kind
your heart sails above us all, your soul
perfect in that it feels everything

down here
so lucky i am to know you
lucky
we are to know your name
charmed
to be yours, i am
this world is
so yours
so so yours
lucky